P9-DVK-908

WISE SAYINGS FROM THE ORIENT

....

ILLUSTRATED BY
MARY JANE GORTON

....

PETER PAUPER PRESS
MOUNT VERNON
NEW YORK

WISE
SAYINGS
FROM THE
ORIENT

·····················

WISE SAYINGS FROM THE ORIENT

ADVICE

The proverb is made for those who take advice.

First think and then act.

If advice enters into one ear of the simpleton, it escapes through the other.

If traveling in the land of the one-eyed, put out one of thy eyes.

Seven thou shalt not neglect: thy wife as long as she lives in peace with thee, thy livelihood as long as it provides for thee, thy ornament as long as it adorns thee, thy friend as long as he is just to thee, thy table companion as long as he understands thee, thy son as long as he cannot take care of himself, and thy guest as long as he does not molest thee.

To every mouth its own spittle tastes sweet. (Every one deems his own advice the best.)

The corruption of the people originates in the corruption of the leaders.

Too many monks destroy the church.

Be not conceited; if a fool tells thee thou hast a pearl in thy hand, know that it is mud.

He leads better than the hand of a man to his mouth. (He is a good adviser.)

Be mad; the whole world is but madness.

A fool gives a nut to him who has no teeth. (He gives advice to one who has not the means to follow it.)

He who takes the raven for a guide will be led to the carcasses of dogs.

A thing to which the fool does not consent, know as the right thing.

He has his spoon in every pot. (He is a meddlesome adviser.)

He who meddles in what does not concern him, what concerns him will escape him.

Love takes no advice.

He who lives on medicine dies of sickness.

A learned man who gives good advice to others and forgets of himself is to be compared with the wick of a lamp which spends light to others, while its own self wastes away.

Every one is most experienced in his own profession.

Keep to custom, and do not break custom.

BUSINESS

Nothing is for nothing, even if the pasha were thy brother.

Drachms collect drachms.

The glory of the merchant is in his bag, the glory of the learned is in his book.

Do not transact business with him whom thou lovest, for his love will soon come to an end.

Every one draws the fire to his own cake.

If there were something good in the owl the hunter would not pass it by. (It is an unprofitable business.)

Where there are many hands the lentils get burnt.

CAUTION

Not he who can extricate himself from difficulties is the prudent, but he who cautiously bewares not to intricate himself.

Keep thy door closed and do not suspect thy neighbor.

Light thy lamp before it gets dark.

It is better that thou shouldst guard thy secret than that another one should guard it.

Caution is counted nuts in a tied bag.

Take that what thou hast seen and leave what thou hast heard.

Three should not be lent away: a comb, a tooth brush and a girl.

The prudent takes no poison even if he possesses the antidote.

The wise must regard himself in this world like a sick man, who needs nourishment, but not every food is fit for him.

Three are not to be trusted: the steadiness of a horse, the favor of a king and the faith of women.

8

Do not deem thy speech secure, for ears has the wall; the wall has no ears, but behind it is a man.

Sometimes one crowing kills the cock.

The fool guards himself from everything but from himself.

Slow but sure reaches goal and reward.

He is prudent who reads the secret in the features of the face.

He fled from the wolf and fell into the pit.

Do not reveal thy secret to the apes.

He who puts his hand under his head will find it again.

When fate interferes, caution is in vain.

Do not joke with the noble, for he will feel offended; nor with the vile, for he will become insolent toward thee.

Speak in the night where there is no owl.

If thou send a boy on an important errand, go after him.

He whom a serpent has stung is afraid of a rope.

Mankind consists of two men; one who takes heed, the other of whom heed is taken.

Do not go naked in the street. (Do not divulge thy secret.)

CHILDREN

The mother of the mute knows the language of the mute.

When the son's beard begins to grow shave thy own beard.

When he was a puppy I brought him up; when he became a dog he bit me.

God save us from the sway of boys and the government of women.

Do not confine your children to your own learning, for they were born in another time.

By much falling the child learns to walk.

From the rose proceeds a thorn, from the thorn a rose.

Be submissive in thy childhood that thou mayest be respected in thy old age.

Honor thy father, and thy son will honor thee.

CONTENTION

Anger in debate causes the argument to be forgotten.

For much wood a little fire suffices.

Do not move the fire with a knife. (Do not add strife to strife.)

His excuse is graver than his injury.

Wound, and wound deeply, for after the battle is but peace.

Inflict pain if thou beat; give enough if thou give to eat.

If you can solve the knot with the tongue, do not solve it with the teeth.

If the wind and the sea quarrel the mariner is at peace.

What is sweeter than sweetness? Peace after struggle.

Quarrel is the weapon of the weak.

He who excuses himself without having given offence makes himself suspected of it.

12

He who knows not a thing is opposed to it.

It is good luck for a man if his enemy is wise.

He who accepts the promise of security from an enemy is not free from danger.

A harmless enemy is better than a useless friend.

A smiling enemy is like a colocynth, it has green leaves, but its taste kills.

May the lion devour me but not the dog.

The night is dark and the rams are butting with their horns. (Said of a great calamity.)

Enmity lies hidden in the mind, like the burning coal behind the embers.

Play alone and thou wilt not become angry.

He who plays with a cat must patiently bear its clutches.

We meet him with an elephant's trunk, who meets us with a long nose.

Do not shoot arrows into an iron statue. (Do not contend with him who is stronger than thou.)

14

EDUCATION

He who proves things by experience increases his knowledge; he who believes blindly increases his errors.

Do not teach the bear to throw stones.

Culture of mind adorns the riches of the rich and hides the poverty of the poor.

Experience is the mirror of the mind.

Culture in a man is better than gold.

How many poor are rich in mind, and how many rich are poor in mind.

I know best the soil of my own land.

The people of Mecca know best its streets.

For the blind in mind there is no physician.

We wonder, O bald head, where we should begin to comb thee.

The foot grows and the understanding remains short.

Culture of heart is better than culture of learning.

15

The most effective admonition is the sight of the dead.

Instruction in the time of youth is like the sculpture on a stone.

Genius is like a sword, and experience like the grinding stone.

The remembrance of death is a polish for the soul.

A person without culture is like a body without a soul.

Do not count the day which brings no gain to thee.

Beware of too much laughter, for it deadens the mind and produces oblivion.

FRIENDSHIP

A friendly smile is a key to security and a lamp to benevolence.

Beware of thy enemy once, of thy friends a thousand times.

The flies know the beard of him who sells honey.

Friendship between fathers is relationship between children.

He who seeks for a faultless brother will have to remain brotherless.

A multitude of friends are a help against time.

New things are the best things; old friends are the best friends.

"Oh, my friend, may God bless thee." Said the other, "Take half of the blessing!"

On thy bucket hangs another bucket.

Thy brother is he who relieves thy need.

Who asks more of a friend than he can bestow deserves to be refused.

Wheat among barley. (Good men in bad company.)

Three are known but in three places: The strong in battle, the wise in his anger and the friend in distress.

The fruit of kindness is many friends.

The remedy of sadness is the sight of a brother.

The enemy of thy father, as long as he lives, will never be thy friend.

If thy associate is insane, be thou sensible.

If thy friend is honey, do not lick him up altogether.

Do not buy the enmity of one for the friendship of thousands.

The genius of the prudent is often led to error by the association with the fool. (One fool makes a thousand fools.)

Be not honey altogether, else people will lick thee up; be not bitterness altogether, else they will spit thee out.

He who confers many benefits has many friends.

The most prudent of men is he who is most excused by men.

The visit of a friend is medicine to the sick.

We must not wonder when the fool associates with the fool; we must rather wonder when the sensible inflicts injury upon the sensible.

The hunter must keep company with the hounds.

To refuse in a kind manner is better than to make long promises.

He blows with every wind. (A fickle minded friend.)

Be not moist, else thou wilt be pressed; be not dry, else thou wilt be broken.

A strange dog does not follow thee.

HONOR

The lion is a lion, even if his clutches become blunt; the dog is a dog, even if brought up among lions.

He who blames the noble degrades himself.

Do not sit down in a place where they might command thee, "Get up!"

From the pearl oyster different things than pearls also proceed.

He is not honored whose neighbors are despised, and he is not happy whose brothers are in distress.

Praise is life in death; vituperation is death in life.

He who is present at a meal to which he was not invited deserves to be chased away.

On account of one eye thousand eyes are honored.

Respect him who is prostrated.

Blameable is he who praises himself before men that know him.

A pearl, though small, is better than a stone, though large.

There is a great difference between silver and tin.

The wise man should not be overbearing, nor should he forget his dignity.

The nobility of a land consists in its inhabitants, not in its soil.

He who takes his reward cannot boast of his merit.

A man cannot be blamed for not being of noble origin.

He who is bashful before others but is not so before himself is wanting in self respect.

Dignity does not consist in a silk dress.

Visit a man according to the honor he does thee.

A lady with two servants, and two eggs in the frying pan. (Poor and Proud.)

Man is to be known by the place where he firmly stands, not where he was planted; by the place where he is found, not where he was born.

He who disdains his riches honors himself.

A lie is shame, truth is honor.

Every stone has its price.

Be no boaster, for those that know thee will despise thee.

Nothing lasts with time except a good or bad name.

Riches perish, a good name lasts.

If my stomach were of glass I would eat every day a cock.

He whose house is the grave should not speak much. (Humility behooves the child of dust.)

Be always among the first, even if it be only in shaving the beard. (Said of one who aspires to honors without possessing merits.)

Water is the most indifferent thing as long as we have it, the most precious as soon as we want it.

Respect him who is above thee.

An ass tied to the sun. (A fool in high station.)

Joke decreases reverence.

From fear of degradation men become degraded. (They seek honor in a way that dishonors them.)

HOUSE

Two in one coffin, but not two in one house.

The guest of the avaricious will not suffer of indigestion.

Gold is an ornament for women.

His stature is the stature of a mouse, and his voice fills the house.

In matrimony is the honey of a month and the thorn of years. (Of unfortunate domestic life.)

O, my neighbor! thou art in thy house, and I am in mine.

How good were the wedding were not the costs.

Do not put the dove and the peacock together in one cage. (Refers to the harem.)

Avarice and ignorance with humility are better than learning and liberality with pride.

The sparrow does not prey in his own nest.

Visitor in the evening, didst thou come to stay over night or to take supper with us? (Said of inopportune visitors.)

Too much visiting engenders tediousness.

On entering every one feels embarrassed; the remedy is a friendly greeting.

The visitor is in the power of him whom he visits.

INCLINATION

Prudence appears in two things: in moderation when we are angry, and in forgiveness when we have the power to punish.

A channel leads from heart to heart.

Man is composed of water and of mud; now he is disturbed, now he is clear.

24

A man is not perfectly wise unless he is able to control his passions.

The heart like the garment gets worn out.

Birds descending to earth flock to their associates.

As the man is so are his tools.

Nothing is harder for a lover than the heartlessness of the beloved.

Do not command the orphan not to weep.

His heart is like the willow; though cold it kindles fire.

Love is the fruit of modesty.

Love is nothing else but the occupation of an idle heart.

A soft branch breaks not.

If the sword were married it would not cut.

Envy is like rust on iron, that leaves it not until it corrodes it.

To be inclined to anger is in the nature of boys; to mourn the past is in the nature of women.

Wine makes that appear what is in man's heart. (*In vino veritas*. When the wine enters, the secret goes out, says the rabbinical proverb.)

Woman becomes fat from the ear. (Female curiosity.)

Patience assures thy victory.

The day of parting is harder than the day of battle.

How far the Pleiades are from the earth!

Love is blind.

Do not say to the singer: "Sing."

The witness of the dog is his tail.

If there were anything good in cabbage, the dog would eat it.

Every wood has its smoke.

Every heart has its own concerns.

Water in the eye is a sign of fire in the heart.

Man is to be known by what he proposes.

The envious is to be known by his being afflicted when another is rejoicing.

Respect is the confirmation of love.

Withstand thy own heart and thou wilt enjoy peace.

Separation was made only to annoy lovers.

Three things produce love: Culture of mind, modesty and meekness.

The thief eats in the house of the robber.

Who loves thee scolds thee.

To accept excuse shows a good disposition of heart.

The spider is from its birth a weaver.

The motion of the eyes shows what passes in the soul.

The cake is not from this dough.

With what the shoe is lined nobody but God and the shoemaker knows.

Water removes all sorrow. (Tears alleviate.)

Do not sleep among graves lest thou have bad dreams. (Him who sleeps in the graveyard the rabbinical phrase calls insane. The general meaning of the proverb is, not to be inclined to melancholy.)

The beginning of anger is madness, the end penitence.

Were it not for patriotism, sterile lands would be deserted.

What the eye does not see, that the heart does not mourn.

Men find a way in that which they love. (Where there is a will, there is a way.)

Sometimes we suspect the heart, even if the tongue be truthful.

The color of the water makes the color of the vase.

Everything has its secret; the secret of wine is joy. (A play of words: *sarro*, secret, and *surur*, gladness.)

Men are the children of this world, and a man cannot be blamed for loving his mother.

28

JUSTICE

That what is for the lawyer he writes down, and what is against him he strikes out.

A lion breaking bones is better than an unjust governor.

A prince without justice is like a cloud without rain.

A prince without justice is like a stream without water.

An unjust judge is like salt on a raw wound.

Do unto thy brother as thou wouldst have him do unto thee.

Exceptions have no rule.

Do not hurt and thou wilt not be hurt.

Thou hast cooked it well, swallow now and taste. (Bear the consequences of thy action.)

Thy right hand shall not inflict injury upon thy left hand. (Be just to thy own kind.)

Treat thy subordinate with kindness, thy equal with justice and thy superior with prudence.

The judge should not hear the complaint of a party unless the accused party is present. (Coincides with the rabbinical principle.)

For what the rain spoils it compensates.

Every lawyer must have his fool.

He who sees his own faults is too much occupied to see the faults of others.

He who is not satisfied with the rule of Moses, will have to be satisfied with the rule of Pharao.

If men would act justly, the judge would enjoy rest.

Where the vile sway, the noble perish.

His own deeds are attributed to every man, and according to what he has done he is recorded.

For every patient a remedy grows among the plants of his own land.

Everything has two ends and a middle; the middle agrees most with justice.

Every tentpole gets its rain. (God provides for the necessaries of every household.)

Men are inclined to him who is inclined to justice.

Every work bears its fruit; either reward or punishment.

A reign with unbelief can last, but with injustice it cannot last.

Be to everyone like a scale. (Just to all.)

Nothing that comes from heaven is more bitter than the cup of blindness.

If the sickness is sent by Heaven then all remedy is in vain.

If thou prohibit a thing, begin with thy own self.

LABOR

For three things there is no remedy: Poverty associated with laziness, sickness coupled with old age, and enmity mixed with envy.

A thing that is spoiled in the beginning ends crooked.

Hard to a man is that to which he is not accustomed.

If thou canst not reach the entire thing do not give it up entirely.

None weeps for thee but thy own eyelid, none shivers for thee but thy own nail. (Self is the man.)

He who does not destroy does not build.

With thy own hand draw out thy thorn.

One man catches the fishes and another man eats them.

The difficulty of a thing is the introductory part to its enjoyment.

Weakness married laziness and their progeny was poverty.

Industry breaks the chain of poverty.

Man flies with his plans as the bird flies with its wings.

Tie strongly what thou tiest.

You have eaten the pistach nut and we shall bother with the shell?

Every work finds its man.

None will scratch my back but my own nail, and none will hasten my business but my own foot.

The following are good when joined together: Learning joined with the fear of God, memory with genius, beauty with kindness, nobility of descent with good morals, joy with security, riches with contentment, and endeavor with the help of God.

A dog has torn it and a dog will eat it. (Said of useless labor.)

The distaff is the best play for women.

Easy for the looker-on is that which passes on the back of the flogged.

Every hand has what it acquires.

He who fatigues his body brings peace to his mind.

Thou strikest a cold iron. (A useless labor.)

You have eaten the dates, and the stones are thrown at me.

Sometimes the one who has the use of his eyes misses the road, and the blind finds the straight path.

On the day of resurrection the ink of the learned will be weighed with the blood of the martyrs.

34

He is like the ostrich, neither carrying nor flying. (To be uncertain between two things.)

Drop added to drop makes the lake.

Man is proved by deeds, not by his words.

LEARNING

If the ignorant would know his ignorance he would not be ignorant.

A man's art is his treasure.

He who knows nothing about architecture wonders at a dovecote.

Knowledge without good deeds is like a tree without fruit.

Knowledge that does not make thee better is an error, and riches that do not help thee are a detriment.

Practice is the fruit of theory.

Quarrel is the weapon of the weak.

Thy brother has cooked it well, but he has dropped it into the ashes. (To spoil a good beginning.)

The fruit of wisdom is peace, and the fruit of riches is fatigue.

Two are not to be satiated; he that seeks knowledge and he that seeks riches.

The beginning of learning is silence, then comes hearing, then writing, then work, then promulgation.

Ignorance is the worst companion.

The learned knows the ignorant, for before he was learned he himself was ignorant; the ignorant, however, does not know the learned, for he never was learned.

What is in the pot wastes, what is in the mind remains.

The world is ruled by the pen.

The men of genius in a generation depend on the time in which they live.

The best company is a good book.

The error of the learned is like a wrecked ship, it sinks, and many are lost with it.

The hardest thing for man is to know himself.

The sieve retains the bran and passes through the flour. (The Mishna distinguishes four classes of pupils: The sponge is he who indiscriminately sucks up everything; the funnel, what he heard enters through one ear and leaves through the other; the strainer retains the dregs and lets the wine escape; the sieve is the discriminating one who knows how to separate the bran from the fine flour. In the above proverb the sieve occupies the place of the strainer in the rabbinical classification.)

A man does not cease to be a genius until he makes a poem or writes a book.

The tribute to learning is teaching.

Beauty is the wisdom of women, and wisdom is the beauty of men.

Riches and all worldly things perish, good deeds remain.

Knowledge is like a hill, hard is the ascent but easy the descent.

He who often remembers his teachers, does not forget what he has learned, and acquires what he does not know.

Everything in profusion is of low value except genius.

To him that cultivates science, science becomes a necessity.

The learned does not cease to exist. (The rabbinical phrase says of the learned: "His lips move in the grave." He speaks even if dead; his opinions and decisions are recited in the school.)

Long beard, short sense.

Meekness is the perfection of learning.

One day of the learned is better than all the life of the ignorant.

Theory without practice is like a cloud without rain.

Do not ride a strange horse. (Do not boast of a knowledge which thou dost not possess.)

OPPORTUNITY

The fox favored by fortune conquers the lion favored by strength.

You give us wine to drink, how can you expect prudence of us?

What is good for the liver is bad for the spleen.

What is the good of a sheath where there is no sword?

Seize the opportunity before its anger returns.

When thy neighbor shaves his beard, soap thou thine.

Eating and flight are not done on purpose.

Opportunity passes like a cloud.

Strike the iron while it is hot.

Hasten with what thou hast to slaughter as long as it is fat.

He bears the child on his shoulders, and is at a loss where to find it.

Not every one who searches finds, and not every one who flees escapes.

Sometimes even the hyacinth finds no buyer.

RICHES AND POVERTY

O, that we had from every thornbush one leaf! (A little from so much.)

A rich miser is poorer than the liberal poor.

He who buys bread with borrowed money, have compassion on him; he who buys meat with borrowed money, throw at him a stone.

A poor man is like a lamp without oil.

He blackened his face for nothing. (Said of one whose request is not granted.)

Better poverty than ill gained riches.

Get up early and thou wilt be prosperous.

Neither fat nor wool. (Said of an entirely worthless thing.)

Poverty without debt is a fortune.

The avaricious is the guardian of his riches and the treasurer of his heir.

Poverty comes from God, but not dirt.

Three make lean — a slow messenger, a lamp that does not shine, and the expectation to dine at the table of him who is yet to come.

What the slave possesses belongs to his master. (Coincides with the rabbinical law.)

Who beats the cymbal before a stable door? (Casting pearls before the swine.)

We do not envy you your roast and cake, and you envy us our sleep in the street. (Said of the rich who envy the poor.)

Beauty of the body is half a fortune.

Thy poor neighbor will make thee poor, and he will not become rich.

The cure for a poor lover is the gold mine.

If thou art forced to beg, knock at the door of the rich.

Satiety hardens the heart.

He who is drowned is not troubled by the rain.

The rich man is great in every one's eyes.

Avarice is not my inclination, but I have nothing wherewith to be liberal. (Poor people are kind hearted.)

Better poverty with security than riches with fear.

Besides the house nothing is in the house. (Utter poverty.)

When the rich man tells a lie all say, "It is true"; and when he dances all say, "How beautiful it is!"

Riches are like water in the house, whose channels are obstructed; if it finds no exit it drowns the owner.

What is the good of a sun that does not warm me? (A possession that one cannot enjoy.)

He who cleans his garment has little care.

He who sleeps knows not of him who is awake.

SATISFACTION

Do not relinquish the little that thou art able to accomplish for the much that thou art not able to accomplish.

A little bitterness spoils much sweetness.

Be liberal with much and contented with little.

Bread is the nourishment that never dies.

He whose mind is after the sea despises the channel.

The provisions for two suffice for three.

To husband the thing that thou possessest is better than to expect what thou desirest.

The little that comes to thee is better than the much to which thou must go.

Secure sleep is the softest bed.

The egg of today is better than the hen of to-morrow.

If thou hast not what thou desirest, desire what thou hast.

Who postpones his breakfast till supper time, over him the enemies will not rejoice.

Every bird rejoices in its own voice.

He who is most necessary to men can most easily dispense with men.

It is better to eat a little of obnoxious food than too much of that which is toothsome.

Abstinence is a tree; its root is satisfaction, and its fruit is quietude.

According to the length of thy mantle stretch out thy feet. (Live according to thy means.)

He who has covetousness as a sumpter will have poverty as a companion.

Soft ground sucks up its own and other water.

He who is abstemious in worldly things rules them; but he who desires them is their slave.

Every bean rejoices in its own blossom.

Every bird finds sufficient prey.

The greatest delight for the inhabitants of Paradise is the consciousness that it will not end.

The envious have no rest in this world.

From plenty does not come blessing, but from blessing comes plenty.

‖‖

SIN
‖‖

Health is better than medicine; not to sin is better than to be forgiven.

One is the thief and many are the suspected.

One crime is too much and a thousand good deeds are too few.

A face without bashfulness is like a log whose bark has been peeled off, and like a lamp whose oil has been consumed.

The garment of the unjust in this world is vituperation, and in the world to come repentance.

He came to bake his fishes in the conflagration. (This proverb is used by the inhabitants of Bagdad of one who conceals his bad intentions; it has its origin in the following: At a conflagration a thief came to steal, and when caught he said, "I came to bake my fishes.")

The fruit of unrighteousness is repentance.

Habit removes bashfulness.

He who repents his sins is as if he had never sinned.

He who steals an egg will steal a camel.

If thy trouble is in good works, know, the trouble will pass and the good works remain; if thy pleasure is in sin, know, the pleasure will pass and the sin remain.

Be not of those who publicly curse the devil, and secretly serve him.

Foul works find foul men.

More deceitful than the vapor at noon tide in the desert. (It has the appearance of water; the thirsty wanderer hastens toward it and finds himself sorely disappointed.)

Envy, hypocrisy and lie are the tripode of villainy.

SPEECH AND SILENCE

A wound inflicted by speech is more painful than a wound inflicted by the sword.

Beware of a speech which came through many witnesses.

Do not trust him who lies for thee, for he is as ready to lie against thee.

Do not traduce the well from which thou hast drunk.

Eloquence consists in making the speech comprehensible to the multitude and agreeable to the learned.

Four cannot be revoked: the spoken word, the arrow, the divine decree, and the past time.

Little rain from a thundering cloud. (To promise much and to do little.)

The lie is not nice unless it comes from the poet.

To lie is the quality of the hypocrite.

Restrain thy tongue always, except in four things: in telling the truth, in refuting the lie, in thanking for benefits and in uttering a word of wisdom.

Three things are repugnant to prudence: a quick answer, wishing too much, and laughing immoderately.

A lie is an evil and truth is its remedy.

To act against a given promise is not the same as to refuse.

Thy secret is thy prisoner if thou keepest it; thou art its prisoner if thou divulgest it.

Speech is a beautiful net in which souls are caught.

The heart of the fool is in his tongue; the tongue of the prudent is in his heart.

The speech of a king is the king of speech.

The public affair of the prudent is a secret; the secret of the fool is a public affair.

When truth rises it repels the lie.

To hear much is convenient, to ask much becomes tedious.

Every place has its word, and every place has its circuit. (A right word and a word of evasion.)

The heart of the liar lies more than his tongue.

50

Turn aside your ears that they may not hear objectionable words. (The rabbis say: Why is the flap of the ear soft? That one may press it into the cavity of the ear when he hears objectionable words.)

Grammar of speech is like salt in food.

The prudent confirms his word by a proverb, the fool by an oath.

Speech is silver, silence is gold.

Do not say No after thou hast said Yes. (The rabbinical phrase: Let thy yes be a yes, and thy no a no.)

Whispering is malevolence.

I have never repented my silence, but often my speech.

The liar has a short rope.

A kind word is the tie of hearts.

Proverbs are the lamps of speech.

He is mixed with water. (Said of the liar.)

When a man despairs, his tongue becomes long.

The bad condition of a speaker shall not hinder thee from listening to his words, for many a deformed mouth imparts correct knowledge. (The rabbinical phrase is: Accept the truth from whosoever utters it.)

Every speech has its answer.

Thy secret is thy blood, do not diffuse it.

A mute tongue is better than a lying tongue.

Silence is the brother of assent.

Thy tongue is like a lion; if thou chainest it, it watches thee, if thou loosenest it, it tears thee in pieces.

Where wisdom is perfect there the words are few.

STRENGTH AND POWER

The friend of a king is like one that rides on a lion; men fear him, and he fears the animal on which he rides.

A body without pain is like a capital on which the taxes are not paid.

Prudence conquers what hosts cannot conquer.

According to the weight of his body the feet of the elephant are made. (God lays not more on a man than he can bear.)

Strength lies in mind not in name.

He who administers to a king should enter blind and leave mute.

A prince is he who knows no prince.

Two that are of the same opinion can conquer a city.

The meanest action in the powerful is to take revenge.

The lion feeds but on his prey.

He was a knee and has become an arm. (Said of one who has suddenly grown powerful.)

Were it not for fear, death and poverty, man would not submit to anything.

Man proposes, God disposes.

It is not evidence of strength in a man to throw himself into an abyss.

He who bears himself proudly in his government will be despised when he is removed from it.

A firm purpose of the soul is strength; uncertainty in council is weakness.

There are times when flight is victory.

If God guards thee, none can harm thee.

He eats the elephant and is choked by a fly.

A cock of a month conquers a hen of a year.

Kiss the hand which thou canst not bite.

Not every one who is covered with a leopard skin is a hero.

The prince of a people is its servant.

Strength and means are the best help.

The king has no brother, the envious has no rest, and the liar has no virtue.

Swords without men are of no use.

Men keep to him who stands.

When the hawk grows old the sparrows mock him.

Two are to be pitied, the noble in the power of the vile, and the wise in the power of the fool.

55

TIME

Thy morning time is a fox, thy evening a wolf. (In youth we are beguiled by time; in old age we are devoured by it.)

When the dust passes thou wilt see whether thou ridest a horse or an ass.

Every moment of time carries away a part of thy life.

How short is the night to him who sleeps.

Number the waves of the sea; those which come are more than those which are gone.

The night covers but day discovers. (German: *Es ist nichts so fein gasponnon, es kommt doch an das Licht der Sonnen.*)

The end of gladness is the beginning of sadness.

Take from death before it takes from thee.

The well lasts longer than the rope.

Upon a full stomach an empty stomach must surely follow.

When the head grows gray the garment is worn out. (The body becomes weak.)

The cup of death makes the round by all, extinguishing even nations.

Birth is a message of death.

Three do not afford security: the sea, a king and time.

When the rose comes the cold goes.

The shining full moon is more beautiful than the darkness.

The coolness of spring increases the roses.

Time consists of two days — one for thee, the other against thee.

The remembrance of youth is a sigh.

Time takes what it gives and disperses what it gathers.

Man is the child of his day; let him, therefore, awake from his dream!

He who runs a race with time hurts his foot.

How many green branches will be charcoal in the morning.

There is no doubt but the seed will be mowed.

He who is older than thou with a day is wiser than thou with a year. (The experience of one day gives sometimes the wisdom of a year.)

After every day follows a night.

Old age is sickness enough.

Man is the servant of time, and time is the enemy of man.

Man may trust his grave but not his time.

The day of joy is short.

If time does not go with thee as thou wishest, go thou with time as he requires.

No hour of thy yesterday passed but it carried part of thy soul away.

Every time has its own men.

Men eat greedily; more greedily, however, time eats them.

Every beginning has an end.

Everything has its nourishment; the nourishment of death is man.

The nearest thing is death and the remotest hope.

The light of the morning renders the light of the lamp useless. (The rabbinical phrase is, "Of what use is the candle at noontime?")

The intoxication of youth is stronger than the intoxication of wine.

Do not count the day which bringeth no gain for thee.

The night hides all calamities.

Every morning has its morning drink.

Of him who is dying few are envious.

He who trusts in time is deceived by it, and who bears himself proudly against it is depressed by it.

VIRTUE AND PIETY

Benefits conferred deem small even if they be great; benefits received deem great even if they be small.

A little bread is better than a thousand words.

One drachm given from religious motives is not equalled by thousands given by command.

Bad morals destroy what the ancestors have built.

59

Conceal thy righteousness as thou concealest thy unrighteousness.

Confer benefits, even if it is on a dog.

With him whose heart is large, his God is satisfied.

If there were no bread, there would be no worship of God. (Gratitude is the root of religious feeling.)

I wonder that he who knows that he must surely die can be glad; I wonder that he who knows that God decrees things can be sad.

If thou hast proposed a thing, trust in God.

One hour to thy own heart and one hour to thy Master.

Provide thy soul with the wholesome food of good works.

Prudence without good morals is a shame, good morals without prudence is a misfortune.

To abstain from the prohibited is better than to seek after the permitted.

The heart of the believer is his leader.

The garment of righteousness never wears out.

60

The perfection of forgiveness is not to mention the suffered wrong.

Were benevolence a creature, man could not see anything more beautiful than she.

The best of men is he who sees his own faults and does not see the faults of others.

The ingenious man without morals is like the strong man without weapons.

There is no piety with avarice.

To give what is not necessary is more than to refuse what is necessary.

The remedy for him who has no remedy is patience.

Impatience is more fatiguing than patience.

Impatience in the unfortunate is the perfection of his calamity.

He who has no sincerity has no religion.

He is the wise man whose action, word, and thought are one and the same.

How many are the fasting who have no other profit from their fast but hunger and thirst?

A sign of thy cleanliness, O youth, is if white garments cover thee in winter time. (The rabbinical adage: Happy our youth that it did not confer shame upon our old age; happy our old age that it does not confer shame upon our youth.)

How many while fasting break their fast; how many while breaking their fast are fasting?

Generous is he who conceals his generosity, so that his left hand knows not what his right hand confers.

Death brings to the righteous rest, and the death of the wicked brings rest to mankind. (The rabbinical proverb says: The sleep of the wicked is good for them and good for the world.)

No garment is more beautiful than righteousness.

Do not allow to thyself what thou dost not allow to others.

By prudence good success is gained; by wisdom evil is restrained.

The upper hand is better than the lower hand. (Better to give than to receive.)

Riches and all worldly things perish, good deeds remain.